# Poetry from the Masters

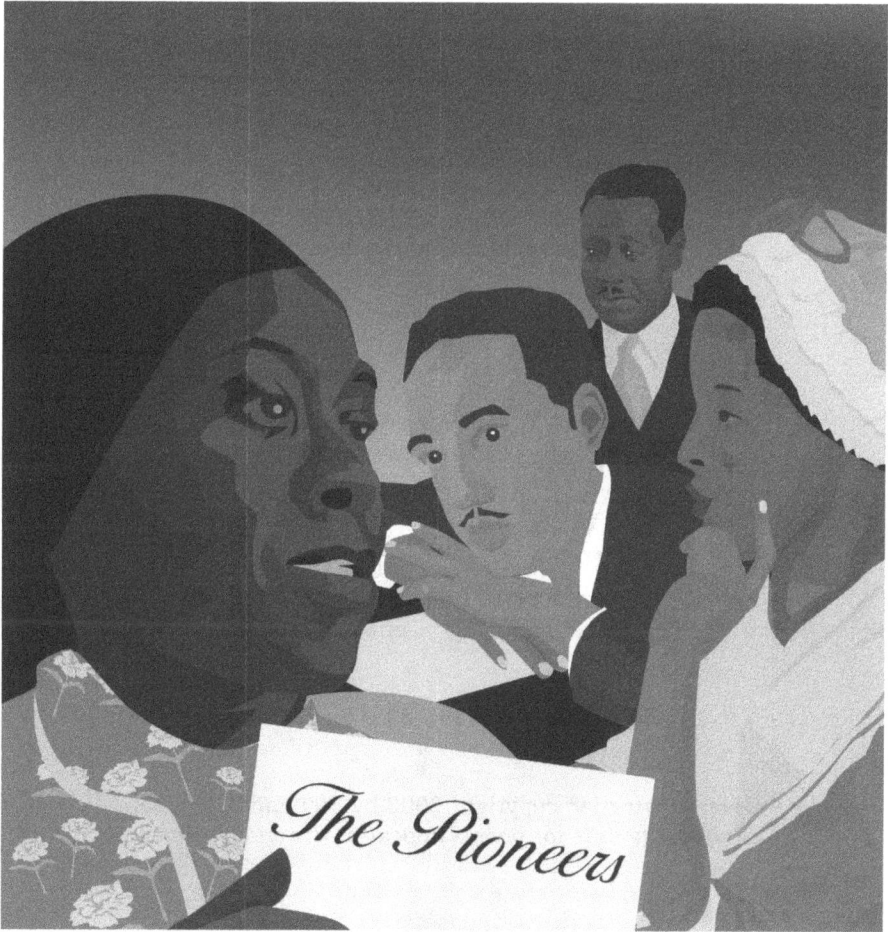

The Pioneers

*An Introduction to African-American Poets*
*edited by Wade Hudson*

For information regarding permission, write to:
Just Us Books, Inc.
P.O. Box 5306
East Orange, NJ 07019
**www.justusbooks.com**

This book is dedicated to all the poets
who just keep writing!

Printed in the USA
12 11 10 9 8 7 6 5 4 3 2
Library of Congress Cataloging-in-publication data is available.

ISBN: 978-1-933491-89-9 (paperback)

# Poetry *from the* Masters
## *The Pioneers*

# Contents

# Introduction

African-American poetry is a barometer of the African-American odyssey. It captures African Americans' highs and lows, and their joy and sadness. Poetry illuminates the anxiety, pain, yearning, hope, faith, and love of a people whose determination to secure freedom and make creative contributions has been unwavering.

Poems written by African Americans have led us in song, rocked us to sleep, inflamed us, made us feel good about who we are, and helped us better understand ourselves and others. Through poetry, one can feel the heartbeat of Black America.

*Poetry from the Masters* is a series that introduces some of the people who helped to create the African-American poetry tradition. This first book, *Poetry from the Masters: The Pioneers*, focuses on those who laid the foundation. They are called the pioneers because they were the trailblazers, the ones who overcame almost impossible obstacles to pave the way for those who came after. Two more books will follow: *Poetry from the Masters: The Black Arts Movement* and *Poetry from the Masters: New Voices*. There are eleven poets featured in *The Pioneers*. Narrowing the list to that number was an extremely difficult job. The poets included in this volume were chosen because of their significant contributions to the African-American poetry tradition. There are others who some might consider worthy of inclusion. But I think very few would question the validity of those who are represented here.

My hope is that young people will read the poems and learn about the lives of the people who wrote them. I also hope that this book will whet readers' appetites and inspire future generations of African-American poets.

—Wade Hudson

# An Overview

The African-American poetic tradition began in the early years of America's history when most African Americans were held in slavery. In most states, slaves were forbidden by law to read or write. If found with a book by a master or overseer, a slave could be beaten or killed. Many Whites in colonial America believed Blacks were mentally inferior and did not have the capacity to think and create on an intellectual level. This kind of thinking was used to help justify the enslavement of millions of African Americans. So the first African-American poets had to overcome many difficult challenges to put pen to paper. And when they were able to do so, the authorship of their creation was questioned.

Phillis Wheatley, the first African American to have a book published, is one such example. Many Whites could not believe she had written the poems accredited to her. Surely such literary accomplishments could not have been achieved by a Black person, they thought. Those Whites who accepted Wheatley's authorship belittled the poems. Thomas Jefferson expressed their sentiment.

"Religion has produced a Phillis Wheatley," said Jefferson, "but it could not produce a poet; her poems are beneath contempt."

But Phillis Wheatley made her literary contributions, and in doing so became a pioneer African-American poet. Another pioneer poet was Jupiter Hammon. In 1760, Hammon's 88-line poem entitled "An Evening Thought, Salvation by Christ, with Penetential Cries" was published. In 1778 he released the poem "An Address to Miss Phillis Wheatley." Obviously, Hammon, who was a slave on a plantation in Long Island, New York, was aware of the poetry of Wheatley, who was a slave of a wealthy White family in Boston, Massachusetts.

George M. Horton was another contributor to early African-American poetry. A slave who lived on a plantation in North Carolina, he began composing poems before he had learned to read or write. In 1829, he published a volume entitled *The Hope of Liberty*. His last volume, *Naked Genius*, was published in 1865. Wheatley, Hammon, and Horton were strongly influenced by their deep religious beliefs. The style and form they employed were much like those of their White contemporaries.

Between the 1840s and the beginning of the Civil War (1861), a number of African-American poets emerged. Most were a part of the abolitionist movement, and unlike the African Americans who preceded them, most of these poets were free. The poems they created addressed different subjects, but much of their verse was written in protest of slavery. In 1853, James Monroe Whitfield released *America and Other Poems*. In 1854, George Boyer Vashon published *Autographs for Freedom*. That same year Frances Ellen Harper published *Poems on Miscellaneous Subjects*.

Like the African-American poets before them, these poets' writing style was influenced by their White contemporaries. But they were among the first to write about subjects related to the African-American experience.

During the 1890s, a new and different voice emerged. It belonged to Paul Laurence Dunbar. Dunbar took the poetry tradition to a higher level and gave it greater depth. His poetry expressed a sensitivity and understanding of African-American life that was rarely found in poetry. He used Black dialect to capture the aspirations, dreams, shortcomings, and humor of Black America. Through his poems, Dunbar brought the lives of regular African Americans to life, and declared them worthy subjects. Although he wrote poems in standard English, he gained national recognition for the poems he wrote in Black dialect.

The African-American poetic tradition came of age during the Harlem Renaissance of the 1920s and 1930s. During this period, critics began to recognize and appreciate the body of work produced by African Americans. The first anthologies of African-American poetry were published. Poets began to experiment with different forms and began to use language in different ways. Sterling

Brown continued Paul Laurence Dunbar's tradition of using Black dialect to capture the realism of Black life. Langston Hughes integrated elements of jazz and blues in his work as he explored all aspects of Black life. Claude McKay and Countee Cullen used traditional literary forms to comment on the Black experience in ways that had not been achieved before. Melvin Tolson, Jean Toomer, Anne Spencer, William Stanley Braithwaite, James Weldon Johnson, Arna Bontemps, Frank Horne, and Jessie Fauset all made important contributions to the tradition during this period as well.

The two most important poets who followed the Harlem Renaissance were Margaret Walker and Gwendolyn Brooks. In 1942, Walker's first volume of verse, *For My People*, was published as the Yale University Younger Poet's award winner. In 1950, Brooks became the first African-American writer to win a Pulitzer Prize for her volume of poetry, *Annie Allen*. The prolific Langston Hughes continued to write until his death in 1967, amassing an enormous body of work that earned him the unofficial title "Poet Laureate of the Negro Race."

In the 1960s and 1970s, poets of the Black Arts Movement believed that politically relevant poems that offered directions to full Black empowerment were essential. Many were activists as well as poets. Haki Madhubuti, Amiri Baraka, Sonia Sanchez, Mari Evans, and Nikki Giovanni are a few of the prominent poets of this era.

Several independent Black presses gave many of these poets an opportunity to be published. Dudley Randall, a university librarian in Detroit, Michigan, established Broadside Press in 1965. Haki Madhubuti, a leader of the Black Arts Movement, established Third World Press in 1967. It is now the nation's oldest continuously publishing Black press. Lotus Press, another publishing house, was started by Naomi Long Madgett, a veteran poet from Detroit, Michigan.

In recent decades, a number of African-American poets have garnered unprecedented success. Rita Dove served as Poet Laureate of the United States from 1993 to 1995. Maya Angelou wrote and recited the poem "On the Pulse of the Morning" for the 1993 inauguration of President Bill Clinton. Yusef Komunyakaa was the 1994 winner of the Pulitzer Prize in poetry for *Neon Vernacular.*

Other poets have garnered grants and awards and have earned prestigious positions at universities and other institutions because of the quality of their work. These include Michael Harper, Lucille Clifton, Derek Walcott, Audre Lorde, Jay Right, Ishmael Reed, Marilyn Nelson, and Gayl Jones.

Most recently, a younger group has burst onto the scene. Some call the work they produce "spoken word." Others call it performance poetry because it is written to be heard. Reciting their poems in nightclubs, theaters, and libraries, these poets integrate elements from Hip-Hop culture with the performance tradition of Black poets of the 1960s and 1970s. Through the efforts of these poets, a new generation is being introduced to the beauty, power, and endurance of the African-American poetic tradition.

# Poetry from the Masters
## The Pioneers

# Phillis Wheatley
## 1753?–1784

Born in West Africa, Phillis Wheatley arrived in the United States on the slave ship Phillis. She was about seven or eight years old when the ship docked in Boston, Massachusetts, in July 1761. John Wheatley, a wealthy merchant from Boston, bought the frail youngster to be a servant for his wife Susanna. In little more than a year, Wheatley, who was given the name of her master, had learned to speak English. The Wheatleys encouraged her thirst for learning by giving her books to read, including the Bible. She soon began writing.

In 1767, when Wheatley was about thirteen years of age, one of her poems was published in a Rhode Island newspaper. In 1770, she achieved international recognition for a poem she wrote about the death of Reverend

George Whitefield, a popular Methodist evangelist. Then, in 1773, Wheatley became the first African American to have a book published. She actually sailed to England to oversee the publication of *Poems on Various Subjects, Religious and Moral*. When she arrived back in Boston several months later, the Wheatley family emancipated the young slave.

Because most Whites did not believe African Americans had the intellectual ability to write a book, *Poems on Various Subjects, Religious and Moral* required a preface from Wheatley's master verifying that she had indeed written the poems. Eighteen prominent Boston citizens also signed a letter attesting that Wheatley was the author.

In 1775, Wheatley wrote what would become perhaps her most famous poem, "To His Excellency General Washington." She sent the poem to George Washington and he sent a letter in return, inviting her to visit with him. The visit with the man who would become the country's first president occurred a few months later.

In 1778, Wheatley married John Peters, a free African American. Wheatley and Peters lived in poverty during most of their marriage. On December 5, 1784, Phillis Wheatley died. Although she had stopped writing poetry during most of her marriage, she composed several poems in the last months of her life.

Phillis Wheatley's accomplishments were important for several reasons. She was the first African American to have a book published, and was the first African American to have a volume of poetry published. She was also the second female poet of any race to be published in North America.

# An Hymn to the Evening

Soon as the sun forsook the eastern main,
The pealing thunder shook the heavenly plain;
Majestic grandeur! From the zephyr's wing,
Exhales the incense of the blooming spring.
Soft purl the streams, the birds renew their notes,
And through the air their mingled music floats.

Through all the heavens what beauteous dyes are
spread!
But the west glories in the deepest red:
So may our breasts with ev'ry virtue glow,
The living temples of our God below!

Filled with the praise of him who gives the light,
And draws the sable curtains of the night,
Let placid slumbers soothe each weary mind,
At morn to wake, more heavenly, more refined;
So shall the labours of the day begin
More pure, more guarded from the snares of sin.

Night's leaden sceptre seals my drowsy eyes;
Then cease, my song, till fair Aurora rise.

# To S.M., A Young African Painter, on Seeing His Works

To show the lab'ring bosom's deep intent,
And thought in living characters to paint,
When first thy pencil did those beauties give,
And breathing figures learnt from thee to live,
How did those prospects give my soul delight,
A new creation rushing on my sight!
Still, wondrous youth! each noble path pursue;
On deathless glories fix thine ardent view:
Still may the painter's and the poet's fire,
To aid thy pencil and thy verse conspire!
And may the charms of each seraphic theme
Conduct thy footsteps to immortal fame!
High to the blissful wonders of the skies
Elate thy soul, and raise thy wishful eyes.
Thrice happy, when exalted to survey
That splendid city, crowned with endless day,
Whose twice six gates on radiant hinges ring:
Celestial Salem blooms in endless spring.
Calm and serene thy moments glide along,
And may the muse inspire each future song!
Still, with the sweets of contemplation blessed,
May peace with balmy wings your soul invest!
But when these shades of time are chased away,
And darkness ends in everlasting day,
On what seraphic pinions shall we move,
And view the landscapes in the realms above!
There shall thy tongue in heavenly murmurs flow,
And there my muse with heavenly transport glow;
No more to tell of Damon's tender sighs,
Or rising radiance of Aurora's eyes;
For nobler themes demand a nobler strain,
And purer language on the ethereal plain.
Cease, gentle Muse! the solemn gloom of night
Now seals the fair creation from my sight.

## Frances Ellen Harper
### 1825–1911

M other, abolitionist, suffragette, teacher, writer, lecturer, African-American leader. Frances Ellen Harper was all of these. She was one of the leading and most respected voices of both Black America and the women's movement.

Frances Ellen Watkins was born in Baltimore, Maryland, in 1825. Although Maryland was a slave state, both of her parents were free Blacks. By the age of three she was orphaned, and went to live with her uncle William Watkins. Her uncle was a minister, educator, and writer, who ran a school. At the school, Harper received an education that the vast majority of African Americans were forbidden to pursue. She displayed abilities in writing and public speaking during her years there. Harper left the school to work as a domestic.

In 1845, Harper published a small collection of poems called *Forest Leaves*. Around 1850, she became the first female teacher at Union Seminary, a school for Blacks established by the African Methodist Episcopal Church near Columbus, Ohio. A year later, she took another teaching position in Little York, Pennsylvania. There she came into contact with fugitives who had escaped from slavery in the South. In 1853, she moved to Philadelphia, Pennsylvania, to devote herself to the abolitionist movement.

Harper traveled extensively, giving lectures about slavery. Yet she found time to write. "Eliza Harris," a poem she published in 1853, brought her national attention. In 1854, she published *Poems on Miscellaneous Subjects*, which sold over 10,000 copies, and was reprinted three years later. During her lifetime, the collection was reprinted at least twenty times.

When Harper married Fenton Harper in 1860, she had already established herself as an abolitionist speaker and writer. The couple had one daughter. When Fenton Harper died in 1864, Frances continued to lecture around the country and write poetry. Other volumes of poems published include *Moses, A Story of the Nile* (1869); *Sketches of Southern Life* (1872); and *Idylls of the Bible* (1901).

Harper's poetry and other writings focused on the struggle of African Americans and women to secure justice and equality in America. She believed literature should be used to enlighten, prod, and bring changes. She died in 1911 in Philadelphia after a long and distinguished career as a writer and as a leader in the fight for Black equality and women's rights.

# The Slave Mother

Heard you that shriek? It rose
   So wildly on the air,
It seemed as if a burden'd heart
   Was breaking in despair.

Saw you those hands so sadly clasped—
   The bowed and feeble head—
The shuddering of that fragile form—
   That look of grief and dread?

Saw you the sad, imploring eye?
   Its every glance was pain,
As if a storm of agony
   Were sweeping through the brain.

She is a mother, pale with fear,
   Her boy clings to her side,
And in her kirtle vainly tries
   His trembling form to hide.

He is not hers, although she bore
   For him a mother's pains;
He is not hers, although her blood
   Is coursing through his veins!

He is not hers, for cruel hands
   May rudely tear apart
The only wreath of household love
   That binds her breaking heart.

His love has been a joyous light
   That o'er her pathway smiled,
A fountain gushing ever new,
   Amid life's desert wild.

His lightest word has been a tone
    Of music round her heart,
Their lives a streamlet blent in one—
    Oh, Father! must they part?

They tear him from her circling arms,
    Her last and fond embrace.
Oh! never more may her sad eyes
    Gaze on his mournful face.

No marvel, then, these bitter shrieks
    Disturb the listening air:
She is a mother, and her heart
    Is breaking in despair.

# The Slave Auction

The sale began—young girls were there,
  Defenceless in their wretchedness,
Whose stifled sobs of deep despair
  Revealed their anguish and distress.

And mothers stood with streaming
  And saw their dearest children sold;
Unheeded rose their bitter cries,
  While tyrants bartered them for gold.

And woman, with her love and truth—
  For these in sable forms may dwell—
Gaz'd on the husband of her youth,
  With anguish none may paint or tell.

And men, whose sole crime was their hue,
  The impress of their Maker's hand,
And frail and shrinking children, too,
  Were gathered in that mournful band.

Ye who have laid your love to rest,
  And wept above their lifeless clay,
Know not the anguish of that breast,
  Whose lov'd are rudely torn away.

Ye may not know how desolate
  Are bosoms rudely forced to part,
And how a dull and heavy weight
  Will press the life-drops from the heart.

# Bury Me in a Free Land

Make me a grave where'er you will,
In a lowly plain or a lofty hill;
Make it among earth's humblest graves,
But not in a land where men are slaves.

I could not rest, if around my grave
I heard the steps of a trembling slave;
His shadow above my silent tomb
Would make it a place of fearful gloom.

I could not sleep, if I heard the tread
Of a coffle-gang to the shambles led,
And the mother's shriek of wild despair
Rise, like a curse, on the trembling air.

I could not rest, if I saw the lash
Drinking her blood at each fearful gash;
And I saw her babes torn from her breast,
Like trembling doves from their parent nest.

I'd shudder and start, if I heard the bay
Of a bloodhound seizing his human prey;
And I heard the captive plead in vain,
As they bound, afresh, his galling chain.

If I saw young girls from their mother's arms
Bartered and sold for their youthful charms,
My eye would flash with a mournful flame,
My death-pale cheek grow red with shame.

I would sleep, dear friends, where bloated
Might Can rob no man of his dearest right;
My rest shall be calm in any grave
Where none can call his brother a slave.

I ask no monument, proud and high,
To arrest the gaze of the passers by;
All that my yearning spirit craves
Is—*Bury me not in a land of slaves!*

## James Weldon Johnson

*1871–1938*

J ames Weldon Johnson is best known as the author of the lyrics to "Lift Ev'ry Voice And Sing," which his brother put to music. It is recognized as the Negro National Anthem. But Johnson's contributions during the first half of the nineteenth century were far-reaching.

In the preface to the groundbreaking *The Book of American Negro Poetry* published in 1922, he wrote, "A people may become great through many means, but there is only one measure by which its greatness is recognized and acknowledged. The final measure of the greatness of all peoples is the amount and standard of the literature and art they have produced."

Johnson played a major role in helping to lift both the amount and standard of African-American arts and letters. A poet, novelist, lyricist, essayist, critic, newspaper editor, and anthologist, he was also a leader in the struggle for Black equality and justice. The National Association for the Advancement of Colored People (NAACP), one of the nation's foremost civil rights organizations, selected him as the first African American to serve as its executive director.

Johnson proved adept at many styles and forms of poetry during his career. Like Paul Laurence Dunbar, he drew from Black folklore in some of his poetry. His popular *God's Trombones: Seven Negro Sermons in Verse*, published in 1927, utilized Black dialect inspired by the spiritual life of southern Blacks.

James Weldon Johnson was born in Jacksonville, Florida, in 1871. His mother was a schoolteacher and his father was a waiter at a popular hotel. The Johnson family, including younger son Rosamond, lived a middle-class life. Helen Louise Johnson shared her love of English literature and classical music with her sons. James graduated from high school in Jacksonville, and from Atlanta University in Atlanta, Georgia. He returned to Jacksonville in 1894 as a teacher and principal, and became the first African American to pass the Florida bar examination. In 1900, he wrote "Lift Ev'ry Voice and Sing" for a celebration of Abraham Lincoln's birthday. A year later Johnson moved to Brooklyn, New York, and studied drama and literature at Columbia University. While there, he and his brother Rosamond garnered success as a songwriting team. Later he turned to public service and journalism. In 1916, he was named national organizer for the NAACP. He was elected to head the organization in 1920. In 1930, Johnson resigned from his leadership position at the NAACP to accept the Spence Chair of Creative Literature at Fisk University. The position had been created especially for him and he held it until 1938 when he died in a car accident.

James Weldon Johnson's published works include the novel *The Autobiography of an Ex-Colored Man* (1912), *Fifty Years and Other Poems* (1917), *God's Trombones: Seven Negro Sermons in Verse* (1927), and *The Book of American Negro Poetry* (1922).

# The Creation

And God stepped out on space,
And he looked around and said:
I'm lonely—
I'll make me a world.

And far as the eye of God could see
Darkness covered everything,
Blacker than a hundred midnights
Down in a cypress swamp.

Then God smiled, And the light broke,
And the darkness rolled up on one side,
And the light stood shining on the other,
And God said: That's good!

Then God reached out and took the light in his hands,
And God rolled the light around in his hands
Until he made the sun;
And he set that sun a-blazing in the heavens.
And the light that was left from making the sun
God gathered it up in a shining ball
And flung it against the darkness,
Spangling the night with the moon and stars.
Then down between
The darkness and the light
He hurled the world;
And God said: That's good!

Then God himself stepped down—
And the sun was on his right hand,
And the moon was on his left;
The stars were clustered about his head,
And the earth was under his feet.

And God walked, and where he trod
His footsteps hollowed the valleys out
And bulged the mountains up.

Then he stopped and looked and saw
That the earth was hot and barren.
So God stepped over to the edge of the world
And he spat out the seven seas—
He batted his eyes, and the lightnings flashed—
He clapped his hands, and the thunders rolled—
And the waters above the earth came down,
The cooling waters came down.

Then the green grass sprouted,
And the little red flowers blossomed,
The pine tree pointed his finger to the sky,
And the oak spread out his arms,
The lakes cuddled down in the hollows of the ground,
And the rivers ran down to the sea;
And God smiled again,
And the rainbow appeared,
And curled itself around his shoulder.

Then God raised his arm and he waved his hand
Over the sea and over the land,
And he said: Bring forth! Bring forth!
And quicker than God could drop his hand,
Fishes and fowls
And beasts and birds
Swam the rivers and the seas,
Roamed the forests and the woods,
And split the air with their wings.
And God said: That's good!

Then God walked around,
And God looked around
On all that he had made.
He looked at his sun,
And he looked at his moon,

And he looked at his little stars;
He looked on his world
With all its living things,
And God said: I'm lonely still.

Then God sat down—
On the side of a hill where he could think;
By a deep, wide river he sat down;
With his head in his hands,
God thought and thought,
Till he thought: I'll make me a man!

Up from the bed of the river
God scooped the clay;
And by the bank of the river
He kneeled him down;
And there the great God Almighty
Who lit the sun and fixed it in the sky,
Who flung the stars to the most far corner of the night,
Who rounded the earth in the middle of his hand;
This Great God,
Like a mammy bending over her baby,
Kneeled down in the dust
Toiling over a lump of clay
Till he shaped it in his own image;

Then into it he blew the breath of life,
And man became a living soul.
Amen.  Amen.

# O Black and Unknown Bards

O Black and unknown bards of long ago,
How came your lips to touch the sacred fire?
How, in your darkness, did you come to know
The power and beauty of the minstrel's lyre?
Who first from midst his bonds lifted his eyes?
Who first from out the still watch, lone and long,
Feeling the ancient faith of prophets rise
Within his dark-kept soul, burst into song?

Heart of what slave poured out such melody
As "Steal away to Jesus?" On its strains
His spirit must have nightly floated free,
Though still about his hands he felt his chains.
Who heard great "Jordan roll"? Whose starward eye
Saw chariot "swing low"? And who was he
That breathed that comforting, melodic sigh,
"Nobody knows de trouble I see"?

What merely living clod, what captive thing,
Could up toward God through all its darkness grope,
And find within its deadened heart to sing
These songs of sorrow, love, and faith, and hope?
How did it catch that subtle undertone,
That note in music heard not with the ears?
How sound the elusive reed, so seldom blown,
Which stirs the soul or melts the heart to tears?

Not that great German master in his dream
Of harmonies that thundered 'mongst the stars
At the creation, ever heard a theme
Nobler than "Go down, Moses." Mark its bars,
That helped make history when Time was young.

There is a wide, wide wonder in it all,
That from degraded rest and service toil
The fiery spirit of the seer should call
These simple children of the sun and soil.
O black slave singers, gone, forgot, unfamed,
You—you alone, of all the long, long line
Of those who've sung untaught, unknown, unnamed,
Have stretched out upward, seeking the divine.

You sang not deeds of heroes or of kings;
No chant of bloody war, no exulting paean
Of arms-won triumphs; but your humble strings
You touched in chord with music empyrean.
You sang far better than you knew; the songs
That for your listeners' hungry hearts sufficed
Still live,—but more than this to you belongs:
You sang a race from wood and stone to Christ.

# Paul Laurence Dunbar

*1872–1906*

**B**ooker T. Washington called Paul Laurence Dunbar the "Poet Laureate of the Negro race." James Weldon Johnson was a close friend and self-described disciple. Frederick Douglass said Dunbar was "the most promising young colored man in America," and helped to arrange for Dunbar to read his poems publicly.

The first African-American poet to achieve national and international acclaim, Dunbar is best remembered for his use of Black dialect in his poetry. Johnson, who also used Black dialect in some of his poetry, said that in Dunbar's work Black dialect had been given "the fullest measure of charm, tenderness, and beauty."

There were critics of Dunbar's dialect poems. English purists didn't acknowledge dialect or colloquium as a viable form of literary expression. Other critics felt that the use of Black dialect was demeaning to African Americans and catered to racial stereotypes that were being promoted throughout American society. His characters, they believed, simply presented African Americans as "happy and content darkies," the way White society wanted them to remain. Supporters, however, marveled at Dunbar's ability to sensitively capture life among everyday African-American people.

Although Dunbar was noted for his use of Black dialect, the majority of his poems were written in standard English. Some addressed the plight of African Americans. But these poems were never accepted as seriously as Dunbar's dialect poetry.

Paul Laurence Dunbar was born in Dayton, Ohio, in 1872. Both of his parents were former slaves. When Dunbar's mother and father separated, he and his three siblings were raised by their mother who worked as a washerwoman. The family of Orville and Wilbur Wright was one of the families for whom she worked. Dunbar's mother passed on her love for poetry and storytelling to her children. By age six, Dunbar had begun writing and reciting poetry.

Paul Laurence Dunbar attended Dayton Central High School where he was a member of the debating society, editor of the school paper, and president of the school's literary society. He was the only African American in his class. After graduation, he could not afford to attend college, so he got a job as an elevator operator. In 1893, Dunbar self-published his first book of poetry, *Oak and Ivy*. His second book, *Majors and Minors*, was published in 1895 and was reviewed favorably in *Harper's Weekly*. Dunbar's third book of poetry, *Lyrics of a Lowly Life*, published in 1896, brought the young writer national attention. Other volumes include *Lyrics of the Hearthside* (1899), *Lyrics of Love and Laughter* (1903), and *Lyrics of Sunshine and Shadow* (1905). Dunbar also published several collections of short stories: *Folks from Dixie*, *In Old Plantation Days*, and *The Heart of Happy Hollow*.

Paul Laurence Dunbar died in 1906 of complications due to tuberculosis. His many supporters hail his talent as a writer and his contributions to American and African-American literature.

# Sympathy

I know what the caged bird feels, alas!
　　When the sun is bright on the upland slopes;
When the wind stirs soft through the springing grass,
And the river flows like a stream of glass;
　　When the first bird sings and the first bud opes,
And the faint perfume from its chalice steals—
I know what the caged bird feels!

I know why the caged bird beats his wing
　　Till its blood is red on the cruel bars;
For he must fly back to his perch and cling
When he fain would be on the bough a-swing;
　　And a pain still throbs in the old, old scars
And they pulse again with a keener sting—
I know why he beats his wing!

I know why the caged bird sings, ah me,
　　When his wing is bruised and his bosom sore,—
When he beats his bars and he would be free;
It is not a carol of joy or glee,
　　But a prayer that he sends from his heart's deep core,
But a plea, that upward to Heaven he flings—
I know why the caged bird sings!

# We Wear the Mask

We wear the mask that grins and lies,
It hides our cheeks and shades our eyes,—
This debt we pay to human guile;
With torn and bleeding hearts we smile,
And mouth with myriad subtleties.

Why should the world be overwise,
In counting all our tears and sighs?
Nay, let them only see us, while
    We wear the mask.

We smile, but, O great Christ, our cries
To thee from tortured souls arise.
We sing, but oh the clay is vile
Beneath our feet, and long the mile;
But let the world dream otherwise,
    We wear the mask!

# The Poet

He sang of life, serenely sweet,
    With, now and then, a deeper note.
    From some high peak, nigh yet remote,
He voiced the world's absorbing beat.

He sang of love when earth was young,
    And Love, itself, was in his lays.
    But ah, the world, it turned to praise
A jingle in a broken tongue.

# Little Brown Baby

Little brown baby wif spa'klin' eyes,
    Come to yo' pappy an' set on his knee.
What you been doin', suh—makin' san' pies?
    Look at dat bib—you's ez du'ty ez me.
Look at dat mouf—dat's merlasses, I bet;
    Come hyeah, Maria, an' wipe off his han's.
Bees gwine to ketch you an' eat you up yit,
    Bein' so sticky an' sweet—goodness lan's!

Little brown baby wif spa'klin' eyes,
    Who's pappy's darlin' an' who's pappy's chile?
Who is it all de day nevah once tries
    Fu' to be cross, er once loses dat smile?
Whah did you git dem teef? My, you's a scamp!
    Whah did dat dimple come f'om in yo' chin?
Pappy do' know you—I b'lieves you's a tramp;
    Mammy, dis hyeah's some ol' straggler got in!

Let's th'ow him outen de do' in de san',
    We do' want stragglers a-layin' 'roun' hyeah;
Let's gin him 'way to de big buggah-man;
    I know he's hidin' erroun' hyeah right neah.
Buggah-man, buggah-man, come in de do',
    Hyeah's a bad boy you kin have fu' to eat.
Mammy an' pappy do' want him no mo',
    Swaller him down f'om his haid to his feet!

Dah, now, I t'ought dat you'd hug me up close.
    Go back, ol' buggah, you sha'n't have dis boy.
He ain't no tramp, ner no straggler, of co'se;
    He's pappy's pa'dner an' playmate an' joy.
Come to you' pallet now—go to yo' res';
    Wisht you could allus know ease an' cleah skies;
Wisht you could stay jes' a chile on my breas'—
    Little brown baby wif spa'klin' eyes!

# Claude McKay

*1889–1948*

During World War II, Winston Churchill recited a poem to inspire and rally his country in its war against Germany. The poem's defiant tone and call to fight against seemingly insurmountable odds helped it become one of the unofficial rallying cries of the Allied Forces. Entitled "If We Must Die," the poem was written by Claude McKay, often referred to as the first poet of the Harlem Renaissance.

"If We Must Die" was published in the *Liberator* in 1919. Written in response to racial violence against African Americans during that year, it was one of the earliest race-conscious poems of the Harlem Renaissance. Although African Americans are not referred to specifically, "If We Must Die" is considered by some critics to be among the first militant poems of the Harlem Renaissance.

McKay published his most important collection of poetry, *Harlem Shadows*, in 1922. Some critics credit it with ushering in the Harlem Renaissance and showing that racial issues can be viable subjects for serious poetry. *Harlem Shadows* grew out of McKay's desire to place "If We Must Die" in a book. About one-third of the poems in the collection focus on the plight and condition of African Americans.

McKay traveled extensively. In 1922, after the release of *Harlem Shadows*, he went to Russia where he became a celebrity. He also traveled to France, Spain, and Morocco, spending a total of twelve years touring Europe and North Africa. During this time, McKay wrote three novels: *Home to Harlem* (1928), *Banjo* (1929), and *Banana Bottom* (1933), and a collection of short stories, *Gingertown* (1932).

Claude McKay was born in Jamaica in 1889, the youngest of eleven children. At seventeen he became an apprentice to a wheelwright and cabinetmaker, and at nineteen he was hired as a police constable in Kingston, Jamaica. While in Kingston, he was encouraged to write by an English collector of island folklore. In 1912, the collector helped McKay publish two books of poetry, *Songs of Jamaica* and *Constab Ballads*. The latter book won an award from the Jamaican Institute of Arts and Sciences. McKay used the cash grant that came with the award to pay for tuition to Tuskegee Institute. He attended Tuskegee briefly before transferring to Kansas State College. He left for Harlem after two years to continue his writing career.

While in Harlem, McKay worked as a waiter and porter while he continued to write. In 1917, two of his sonnets were published in *The Seven Arts* magazine, garnering him wide recognition. Soon, McKay's poems began to appear in many of the leading magazines of the period, including *Pearson's*, *Crisis*, and *Opportunity*. In 1919, McKay traveled to England where a number of his poems were published in several leading magazines. He returned to New York and continued to write. When *Harlem Shadows* was released in 1922, it received exceptional acclaim.

After McKay returned from his 12-year journey to Europe and North Africa, his writing career waned. He died in 1948 in Chicago, Illinois. A collection of his poems entitled *Selected Poems of Claude McKay* was published in 1953, five years after his death.

# Africa

The sun sought thy dim bed and brought forth light,
The sciences were sucklings at thy breast;
When all the world was young in pregnant night
Thy slaves toiled at thy monumental best.
Thou ancient treasure-land, thou modern prize,
New peoples marvel at thy pyramids!
The years roll on, thy sphinx of riddle eyes
Watches the mad world with immobile lids.
The Hebrews humbled them at Pharaoh's name.
Cradle of Power! Yet all things were in vain!
Honor and Glory, Arrogance and Fame!
They went. The darkness swallowed thee again.
Thou art the harlot, now thy time is done,
Of all the mighty nations of the sun.

# If We Must Die

If we must die, let it not be like hogs
Hunted and penned in an inglorious spot,
While round us bark the mad and hungry dogs,
Making their mock at our accursed lot.
If we must die, O let us nobly die,
So that our precious blood may not be shed
In vain; then even the monsters we defy
Shall be constrained to honor us though dead!
O kinsmen! we must meet the common foe!
Though far outnumbered let us show us brave,
And for their thousand blows deal one deathblow!
What though before us lies the open grave?
Like men we'll face the murderous, cowardly pack,
Pressed to the wall, dying, but fighting back!

# America

Although she feeds me bread of bitterness,
And sinks into my throat her tiger's tooth,
Stealing my breath of life, I will confess
I love this cultured hell that tests my youth!
Her vigor flows like tides into my blood,
Giving me strength erect against her hate.
Her bigness sweeps my being like a flood.
Yet as a rebel fronts a king in state,
I stand within her walls with not a shred
Of terror, malice, not a word of jeer.
Darkly I gaze into the days ahead,
And see her might and granite wonders there,
Beneath the touch of Time's unerring hand,
Like priceless treasures sinking in the sand.

# Harlem Shadows

I hear the halting footsteps of a lass
    In Negro Harlem when the night lets fall
Its veil. I see the shapes of girls who pass
    To bend and barter at desire's call.
Ah, little dark girls who in slippered feet
Go prowling through the night from street to street!

Through the long night until the silver break
    Of day the little gray feet know no rest;
Through the lone night until the last snow-flake
    Has dropped from heaven upon the earth's white breast,
The dusky, half-clad girls of tired feet
Are trudging, thinly shod, from street to street.

Ah, stern harsh world, that in the wretched way
    Of poverty, dishonor and disgrace,
Has pushed the timid little feet of clay
    The sacred brown feet of my fallen race!
Ah, heart of me, the weary, weary feet
In Harlem wandering from street to street.

# Georgia Douglas Johnson

*1886–1966*

During the 1920s and 1930s in Washington, D.C., Saturday nights at Georgia Douglas Johnson's was the place to be. Some of the leading African-American writers and intellectuals of the period frequented the house located at 1461 S Street NW. It was a place where African-American writers could receive encouragement and inspiration from their peers and mentors. Among those who attended these gatherings were Langston Hughes, Countee Cullen, Jean Toomer, Angelina Grimke, Jessie Fauset, and Alaine Locke.

Georgia Johnson was more than a hostess, she was an important writer as well. She began writing in her twenties, after devoting much of her time to her first love, music. Her first published poems appeared in *Crisis* magazine in

1916. Her first collection, *The Heart of a Woman*, was published in 1918. African-American writer and critic William Stanley Braithwaite said of *The Heart of a Woman*, "the poems are intensely feminine and for me this means more than anything else that they are deeply human." Some, however, criticized the collection because it did not address the issue of race. Johnson's second volume, *Bronze: A Book of Verse*, published in 1922, was dedicated entirely to racial themes. *An Autumn Love Cycle*, her third volume of verse published in 1928, is considered by some critics to be her best.

Although best known for her poetry, Johnson also wrote plays, short stories, and a novel. Several of her short stories appeared in *Challenge*, a journal published by Dorothy West, another important female writer from the Harlem Renaissance.

Georgia Johnson was born in Atlanta, Georgia, in 1886. She attended public school in Atlanta and graduated from Atlanta University in 1896. She also studied music at Oberlin College and at the Cleveland College of Music. She taught school for a few years in Georgia. She married Henry Lincoln Johnson in 1903, and in 1910, the Johnsons moved to Washington, D.C. Johnson's husband died in 1925, but she remained in Washington, writing, lecturing, and hosting other writers at the place she called "Halfway House."

Georgia Douglas was the first African-American woman poet to receive national recognition since Frances Ellen Harper. She published her last volume of poetry, *Share My World*, in 1962. In 1965, Atlanta University conferred on her an honorary doctoral degree. Johnson died in 1966. One of her most famous poems, "I Want to Die While You Love Me," was read at her funeral.

# I Want to Die While
# You Love Me

I want to die while you love me,
   While yet you hold me fair,
While laughter lies upon my lips
   And lights are in my hair.

I want to die while you love me,
   And bear to that still bed,
Your kisses turbulent, unspent,
   To warm me when I'm dead.

I want to die while you love me,
   Oh, who would care to live
Till love has nothing more to ask
   And nothing more to give!

I want to die while you love me
   And never, never see
The glory of this perfect day
   Grow dim or cease to be.

# The Heart of a Woman

The heart of a woman goes forth with the dawn,
As a lone bird, soft winging, so restlessly on,
Afar o'er life's turrets and vales does it roam
In the wake of those echoes the heart calls home.

The heart of a woman falls back with the night,
And enters some alien cage in its plight,
And tries to forget it has dreamed of the stars,
While it breaks, breaks, breaks on the sheltering bars.

# Your World

Your world is as big as you make it.
I know, for I used to abide
In the narrowest nest in a corner,
My wings pressing close to my side.

But I sighted the distant horizon
Where the skyline encircled the sea
And I throbbed with a burning desire
To travel this immensity.

I battered the cordons around me
And cradled my wings on the breeze,
Then soared to the uttermost reaches
With rapture, with power, with ease!

# Countee
# Cullen
*1903–1946*

During the beginning of the Harlem Renaissance, no African-American poet seemed to have a more promising career than Countee Cullen, not even Langston Hughes. During that period, Cullen won a number of awards, including the John Reed Memorial Prize from *Poetry* magazine, the Spingarn Award from *Crisis* magazine, and several Witter Byner poetry contests. In 1925, the year he graduated from New York University, Cullen published his first volume of poetry, *Color*. He received the Harmon Foundation Literary Award in 1927 for the anthology of African-American poetry entitled *Caroling Dust*. He published two volumes of poems that year as well, *Copper Sun* and *The Ballad of the Brown Girl: An Old Ballad Retold*. His column "The Dark Tower," which appeared in *Opportunity* magazine, brought him even greater influence When he married the daughter of W.E.B. DuBois in 1928, it was the social event of the year. More than 1,000 people attended the wedding

But after the 1920s, Cullen's literary career waned. He did not enjoy long-term success like Langston Hughes. But he is still remembered as one of the shining stars of the Harlem Renaissance.

Cullen is believed to have been born in Louisville, Kentucky. When he was still a baby, he was left in the care of his grandmother. When she died, the teenager was taken in by Reverend Frederick Cullen, a well-known Harlem minister. An excellent student, Cullen attended public school in New York City. He graduated Phi Beta Kappa from New York University and attended Harvard University where he received a master's degree.

Cullen was influenced by romantic poets like Keats, Shelley, and Wordsworth. He wrote lyrical poems and sonnets and resisted being labeled a "Negro poet." In an interview he said, "If I am going to be a poet at all, I am going to be a poet and not a Negro poet."

Still, some of Cullen's most poignant poems reflected an interest in racial issues. However, unlike Hughes and Claude McKay, who both embraced the causes of the Black masses, Cullen did not feel obligated to write from a Black perspective.

In 1929, Cullen published *The Black Christ and Other Poems*, but it was not well received. Other published works, which included novels and several children's books, did not fare well. Cullen turned to teaching for a while and moved to Chicago, where he died in 1946.

# Heritage

### For Harold Jackman

What is Africa to me:
Copper sun or scarlet sea,
Jungle star or jungle track,
Strong bronzed men, or regal black
Women from whose loins I sprang
When the birds of Eden sang?
*One three centuries removed*
*From the scenes his fathers loved,*
*Spicy grove, cinnamon tree,*
*What is Africa to me?*

So I lie, who all day long
Want no sound except the song
Sung by wild barbaric birds
Goading massive jungle herds,
Juggernauts of flesh that pass
Trampling tall defiant grass
Where young forest lovers lie,
Plighting troth beneath the sky.
So I lie, who always hear,
Though I cram against my ear
Both my thumbs, and keep them there,
Great drums throbbing through the air.
So I lie, whose fount of pride,
Dear distress, and joy allied,
Is my somber flesh and skin,
With the dark blood dammed within
Like great pulsing tides of wine
That, I fear, must burst the fine
Channels of the chafing net
Where they surge and foam and fret.

Africa? A book one thumbs
Listlessly, till slumber comes.

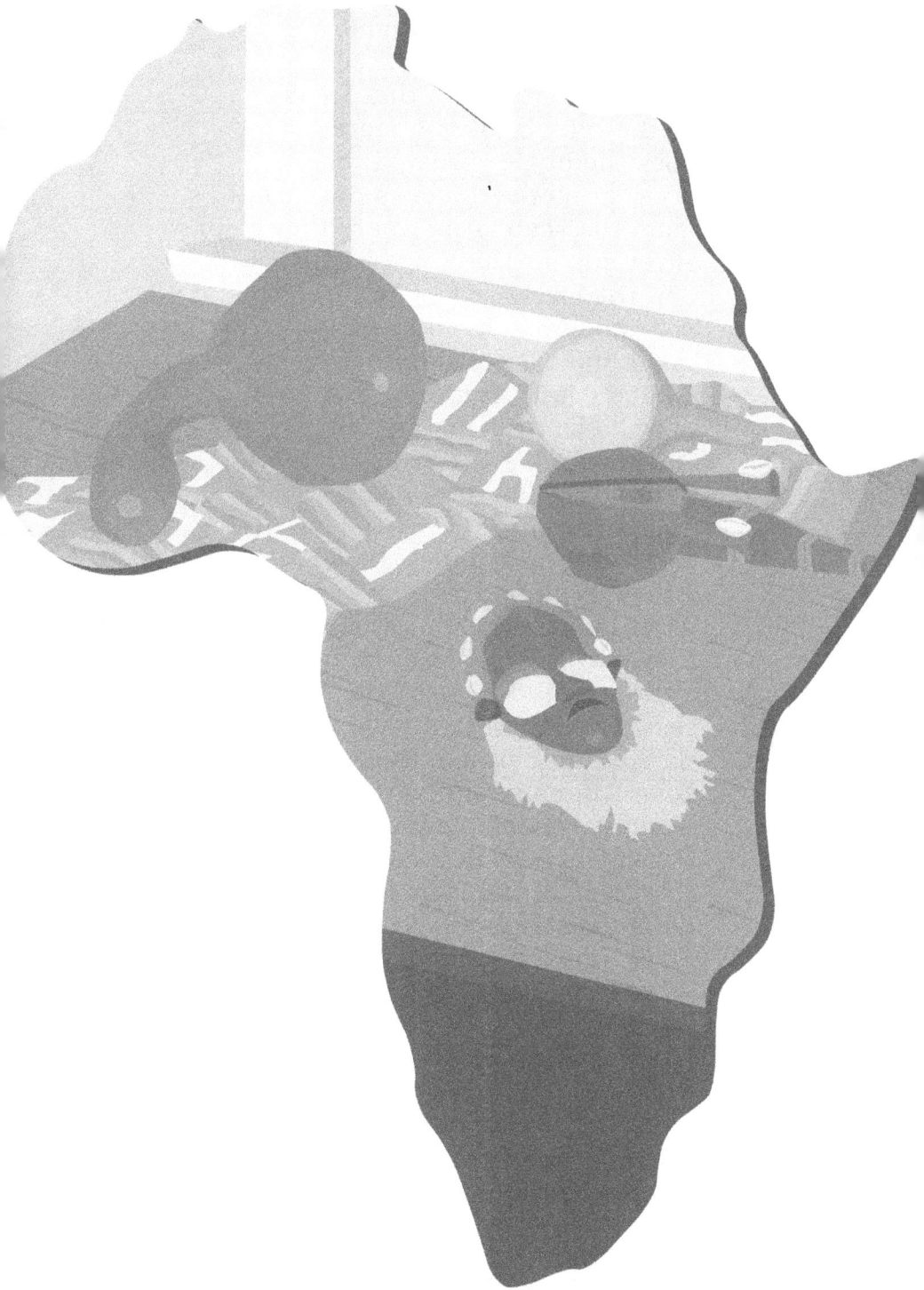

Unremembered are her bats
Circling through the night, her cats
Crouching in the river reeds,
Stalking gentle flesh that feeds
By the river brink; no more
Does the bugle-throated roar
Cry that monarch claws have leapt
From the scabbards where they slept.
Silver snakes that once a year
Doff the lovely coats you wear,
Seek no covert in your fear
Lest a mortal eye should see;
What's your nakedness to me?
Here no leprous flowers rear
Fierce corollas in the air;
Here no bodies sleek and wet,
Dripping mingled rain and sweat,
Tread the savage measures of
Jungle boys and girls in love.
What is last year's snow to me,
Last year's anything? The tree
Budding yearly must forget
How its past arose or set—
Bough and blossom, flower, fruit,
Even what shy bird with mute
Wonder at her travail there,
Meekly labored in its hair.
*One three centuries removed*
*From the scenes his fathers loved,*
*Spice grove, cinnamon tree,*
*What is Africa to me?*

So I lie, who find no peace
Night or day, no slight release
From the unremittant beat
Made by cruel padded feet
Walking through my body's street.

Up and down they go, and back,
Treading out a jungle track.
So I lie, who never quite
Safely sleep from rain at night—
I can never rest at all
When the rain begins to fall;
Like a soul gone mad with pain
I must match its weird refrain;
Ever must I twist and squirm,
Writhing like a baited worm,
While its primal measures drip
Through my body, crying, "Strip!
Doff this new exuberance.
Come and dance the Lover's Dance!"
In an old remembered way
Rain works on me night and day.

Quaint, outlandish heathen gods
Black men fashion out of rods,
Clay, and brittle bits of stone,
In a likeness like their own,
My conversion came high-priced;
I belong to Jesus Christ,
Preacher of humility;
Heathen gods are naught to me.

Father, Son, and Holy Ghost,
So I make an idle boast;
Jesus of the twice-turned cheek,
Lamb of God, although I speak
With my mouth thus, in my heart
Do I play a double part.
Ever at Thy glowing altar
Must my heart grow sick and falter,
Wishing He I served were black,
Thinking then it would not lack
Precedent of pain to guide it,
Let who would or might deride it;

Surely then this flesh would know
Yours had borne a kindred woe.
Lord, I fashion dark gods, too,
Daring even to give You
Dark despairing features where,
Crowned with dark rebellious hair,
Patience wavers just so much as
Mortal grief compels, while touches
Quick and hot, of anger, rise
To smitten cheek and weary eyes.
Lord, forgive me if my need
Sometimes shapes a human creed.
*All day long and all night through,*
*One thing only must I do:*
*Quench my pride and cool my blood,*
*Lest I perish in the flood.*
*Lest a hidden ember set*
*Timber that I thought was wet*
*Burning like the dryest flax,*
*Melting like the merest wax,*
*Lest the grave restore its dead.*
*Not yet has my heart or head*
*In the least way realized*
*They and I are civilized.*

# From the Dark Tower

To Charles S. Johnson

We shall not always plant while others reap
The golden increment of bursting fruit,
Not always countenance, abject and mute,
That lesser men should hold their brothers cheap;
Not everlastingly while others sleep
Shall we beguile their limbs with mellow flute,
Not always bend to some more subtle brute;
We were not made eternally to weep.

The night whose sable breast relieves the stark,
White stars is no less lovely being dark,
And there are buds that cannot bloom at all
In light, but crumple, piteous, and fall;
So in the dark we hide the heart that bleeds,
And wait, and tend our agonizing seeds.

# Incident

For Eric Walrond

Once riding in old Baltimore,
    Heart-filled, head-filled with glee,
I saw a Baltimorean
    Keep looking straight at me.

Now I was eight and very small,
    And he was no whit bigger,
And so I smiled, but he poked out
    His tongue, and called me, "Nigger."

I saw the whole of Baltimore
    From May until December;
Of all the things that happened there
    That's all that I remember.

# Langston Hughes

*1902–1967*

It is virtually impossible to engage in a discussion about the Harlem Renaissance without Langston Hughes's name being introduced early on. For some staunch Hughes supporters, the prolific writer was the Harlem Renaissance. Unlike most writers who emerged during this important period of Black art and culture, Hughes survived the end of the movement. His career as a writer spanned more than four decades, lasting until the 1960s.

Hughes wrote poetry, novels, children's books, plays, short stories, articles, and newspaper columns. He was a prolific writer, whose volume of work is surpassed by very few authors of any race. Unlike some African-American writers who chose to ignore everyday African Americans because they felt them an embarrassment, Hughes was drawn to this major segment of the Black population. He was known for his insightful and colorful portrayals of all aspects of African-American life. Hughes wanted to tell the stories of his people in ways that captured their culture in its entirety. He was especially drawn to jazz and blues and his writing was influenced by both.

Langston Hughes was born James Langston Hughes in Joplin, Missouri. He was a descendant of a distinguished family. His great-uncle was James Mercer Langston, the founding dean of the law school at Howard University. His grandfather was active in politics in Kansas. Langston's mother and father were separated when he was a small boy. He grew up in Lawrence, Kansas; Lincoln, Illinois; and Cleveland, Ohio, where he lived with his mother and her second husband. Following graduation from high school in Cleveland in 1920, he went to live with his father in Mexico. On the train he wrote one of his most popular poems, "The Negro Speaks of Rivers." It was published in the NAACP *Crisis* magazine in 1921.

Hughes's professional career as a published writer had begun months earlier when two of his poems were printed in *The Brownies Book*, a Black children's magazine. A year later, Hughes moved to Harlem to attend Columbia University. But he left because the large university was not for him. He concentrated on his writing and supported himself by working odd jobs. More of his poems were published in literary magazines. In 1923 and 1924 he traveled to Africa and to Europe. While in Paris, he began using the rhythm and spirit of jazz and blues in his poetry. In 1926, Hughes enrolled at Lincoln University, a historically Black institution located in Pennsylvania. During the summers, however, he went back to Harlem. He graduated from Lincoln in 1929.

In 1926, *The Weary Blues*, Hughes's first collection of poems, was published. The poem "The Weary Blues," which won a literary contest sponsored by *Opportunity* magazine in 1925, was the first to make use of the basic blues form.

During his long career, Hughes established a reputation as perhaps the most versatile of all African-American writers. He is often called the "Poet Laureate of the Negro Race," a title he cherished and encouraged. Hughes died in 1967 of complications from prostate cancer. His residence at 20 East 127th Street in his beloved Harlem has been designated a landmark by the New York City Landmarks Preservation Commission, and 20 East 127th Street was renamed "Langston Hughes Place."

# Mother to Son

Well, son, I'll tell you:
Life for me ain't been no crystal stair.
It's had tacks in it,
And splinters,
And boards torn up,
And places with no carpet on the floor—
Bare.
But all the time
I'se been a-climbin' on,
And reachin' landin's,
And turnin' corners,
And sometimes goin' in the dark
Where there ain't been no light.
So boy, don't you turn back.
Don't you set down on the steps
'Cause you finds it's kinder hard.
Don't you fall now—
For I'se still goin', honey,
I'se still climbin',
And life for me ain't been no crystal stair.

# Madam and the Rent Man

The rent man knocked.
He said, Howdy-do?
I said, What
Can I do for you?
He said, You know
Your rent is due.

I said, Listen,
Before I'd pay
I'd go to Hades
And rot away!

The sink is broke
The water don't run,
And you ain't done a thing
You promised to've done.

Back window's cracked,
Kitchen floor squeaks,
There's rats in the cellar,
And the attic leaks.

He said, Madam,
It's not up to me.
I'm just the agent,
Don't you see?

I said, Naturally,
You pass the buck.
If it's money you want
You're out of luck.

He said, Madam,
I ain't pleased!
I said, Neither am I.

So we agrees!

*Poetry from the Masters: The Pioneers*

# Dream Variations

To fling my arms wide
In some place of the sun,
To whirl and to dance
Till the white day is done.
Then rest at cool evening
Beneath a tall tree
While night comes on gently,
    Dark like me—
That is my dream!

To fling my arms wide
In the face of the sun,
Dance! Whirl! Whirl!
Till the quick day is done.
Rest at pale evening . . .
A tall, slim tree . . .
Night coming tenderly
    Black like me.

# The Negro Speaks of Rivers

I've known rivers:
I've known rivers ancient as the world and older than the
   flow of human blood in human veins.

My soul has grown deep like the rivers.

I bathed in the Euphrates when dawns were young.
I built my hut near the Congo and it lulled me to sleep.
I looked upon the Nile and raised the pyramids above it.
I heard the singing of the Mississippi when Abe Lincoln
        went down to New Orleans, and I've seen its muddy
        bosom turn all golden in the sunset.

I've known rivers:
Ancient, dusky rivers.

My soul has grown deep like the rivers.

# I, Too

I, too, sing America.

I am the darker brother.
They send me to eat in the kitchen
When company comes,
But I laugh,
And eat well,
And grow strong.

Tomorrow,
I'll be at the table
When company comes.
Nobody'll dare
Say to me,
"Eat in the kitchen,"
Then.

Besides,
They'll see how beautiful I am
And be ashamed—

I, too, am America.

# Sterling
# Brown
*1901–1989*

Sterling Brown was one of the two major folk poets to emerge during the Harlem Renaissance. The other was Langston Hughes. But after achieving some success as a poet, Brown chose to focus more on his teaching career. For decades he taught in the English department at Howard University, one of the country's most prestigious historically Black universities. Students were drawn to the engaging professor, and he enjoyed sharing his knowledge and experience with them.

*Southern Road*, Brown's first book of poetry, was published in 1932. In his poems, Brown incorporated

African-American folklore and the language of everyday Black people. Although Paul Laurence Dunbar had achieved success first using what was termed Black dialect, most of his poems were sweet or humorous. Only a few of his poems focused on the serious issues that African Americans faced. Brown's poems, however, were frank and brutally honest depictions of African-American life, including racism and discrimination. His passion for jazz and the blues was also prominent in his work, and *Southern Road* established Brown as a serious poet. But many people, including some African Americans, were critical of the use of Black dialect in literature.

Brown was not able to find a publisher for his next collection of poetry. So he began concentrating on teaching, writing literary criticism, and editing poetry anthologies. In 1941, along with Arthur P. Davis and Ulysses Lee, he edited *The Negro Caravan*, one of the most important collections of Black writing ever to be published. His second collection of poetry, *The Last Ride of Wild Bill*, was not published until 1975. In 1980, *The Collected Poems of Sterling A. Brown* was released.

Sterling Brown was born in Washington, D.C. His father was a professor at Howard University. Brown graduated from Dunbar High School, and then attended Williams College in Massachusetts, where he received a bachelor's degree in 1922. He earned a master's degree from Harvard University in 1923.

After teaching at Virginia Seminary and College in Lynchburg, Virginia, for several years, Brown taught at Howard University in Washington, D.C., from 1929 until 1969. In 1971 Howard University awarded him an honorary doctorate degree in recognition of the outstanding contributions he had made to the university and its students.

Sterling Brown died in 1989. But he had seen a renewed interest in his body of work that continues to influence African-American writers today.

# Strong Men

*The strong men keep coming on.*
—Sandburg

*They dragged you from homeland,*
*They chained you in coffles,*
*They huddled you spoon-fashion in filthy hatches,*
*They sold you to give a few gentlemen ease.*

*They broke you in like oxen,*
*They scourged you,*
*They branded you,*
*They made your women breeders,*
*They swelled your numbers with bastards . . . .*
*They taught you the religion they disgraced.*

*You sang:*
   *Keep a-inchin' along*
   *Lak a po' inch worm . . . .*

*You sang:*
   *Bye and bye*
   *I'm gonna lay down dis heaby load . . . .*

*You sang:*
   *Walk togedder, chillen,*
   *Dontcha git weary . . . .*
            The strong men keep a-comin' on
            The strong men git stronger.

*They point with pride to the roads you built for them,*
*They ride in comfort over the rails you laid for them,*
*They put hammers in your hands*
*And said—Drive so much before sundown.*

*You sang:*
        *Ain't no hammah*
        *In dis lan',*
        *Strikes lak mine, bebby,*
        *Strikes lak mine.*

*They cooped you in their kitchens,*
*They penned you in their factories,*
*They gave you the jobs that they were too good for,*
*They tried to guarantee happiness to themselves*
*By shunting dirt and misery to you.*

*You sang:*
        *Me an' muh baby gonna shine, shine*
        *Me an' muh baby gonna shine.*
                The strong men keep a-comin' on
                The strong men git stronger . . . .

*They bought off some of your leaders*
*You stumbled, as blind men will . . . .*
*They coaxed you, unwontedly soft-voiced . . . .*
*You followed a way.*
*Then laughed as usual.*

*They heard the laugh and wondered;*
*Uncomfortable;*
*Unadmitting a deeper terror . . . .*
                The strong men keep a-comin' on
                Gittin' stronger . . . .

*What, from the slums*
*Where they have hemmed you,*
*What, from the tiny huts*
*They could not keep from you—*
*What reaches them*
*Making them ill at ease, fearful?*
*Today they shout prohibition at you*
*"Thou shalt not this"*
*"Thou shalt not that"*
*"Reserved for whites only"*
*You laugh.*

*One thing they cannot prohibit—*
The strong men . . . coming on
The strong men gittin' stronger.
Strong men . . . .
Stronger . . . .

# Rain

Outside the cold, cold night; the dripping rain . . . .
The water gurgles loosely in the eaves,
The savage lashes stripe the rattling pane
And beat a tattoo on November leaves.
The lamp wick gutters, and the last log steams
Upon the ash-filled hearth. Chill grows the room.
The ancient clock ticks creakily and seems
A fitting portent of the gathering gloom.

This is a night we planned. This place is where
One day, we would be happy; where the light
Should tint your shoulders and your wild flung hair.—
Whence we would—oh, we planned a merry morrow—
Recklessly part ways with the old hag, Sorrow . . .

Outside the dripping rain; the cold, cold night.


# After Winter

He snuggles his fingers
In the blacker loam
The lean months are done with,
The fat to come.

His eyes are set
On a brushwood-fire
But his heart is soaring
Higher and higher.

Though he stands ragged
An old scarecrow,
This is the way
His swift thoughts go,

*"Butter beans fo' Clara*
*Sugar corn fo' Grace*
*An' fo' de little feller*
*Runnin' space.*

*"Radishes and lettuce*
*Eggplants and beets*
*Turnips fo' de winter*
*An' candied sweets*

*"Homespun tobacco*
*Apples in de bin*
*Fo' smokin' an' fo' cider*
*When de folks draps in."*

He thinks with the winter
His troubles are gone;
Ten acres unplanted
To raise dreams on.

The lean months are done with,
The fat to come.
His hopes, winter wanderers,
Hasten home.

*"Butter beans fo' Clara*
*Sugar corn fo' Grace*
*An' fo' de little feller*
*Runnin' space . . . ."*

## Margaret Walker
### 1915–1998

argaret Walker's career as a poet was similar to the career of Sterling Brown. Like Brown, Walker found success with her first volume of poetry. Like Brown, decades would pass before she would again have a volume of poetry published. And Walker, like Brown, established an outstanding career as a college educator.

Margaret Walker burst on the literary scene in 1942 when her volume of poetry, *For My People*, was published. The book won the Yale University Younger Poet's Award and received good reviews from many literary critics. American writer Stephen Vincent Benét, who wrote the introduction to *For My People*, was impressed by the power and controlled intensity of the work. "These poems keep on talking to you after the book is shut because . . . Walker has made living and passionate speech," Benét wrote.

More than twenty years would pass before Margaret Walker would again be published. She turned to education, teaching English at Livingstone College in North Carolina, West Virginia State College, and finally at Jackson State College, in Mississippi, where she remained for more than twenty years.

Walker was born in Birmingham, Alabama. She was exposed to the classics of English and American literature at an early age. While a student at Northwestern University in Illinois, she worked for the Works Progress Administration (WPA) Federal Writers' Project, where she became friends with novelist Richard Wright. The WPA was a work-relief agency created in 1935 during the Depression to preserve individuals' skills and self-respect by providing useful work. Walker also assisted Wright with the research for his famous novel *Native Son*. While at the University of Iowa Writers' Workshop she finished *For My People*.

Walker made her return to the literary world in 1966 when her novel *Jubilee* was published. A fictionalized story of her great-grandmother's experiences during slavery and Reconstruction, the book won a Houghton Mifflin Literary Award. Several volumes of poetry followed: *The Ballad of the Free* (1966), *Prophets for a New Day* (1970), *October Journey* (1973), *Far Farish Street Green, February 27, 1986* (1986) and *This Is My Century: New and Collected Poems* (1989). The first three books were published by Broadside Press, a Black-owned publishing company headquartered in Detroit, Michigan. Walker felt it was extremely important that she supported Black independent publishers dedicated to giving a voice to Black America. In 1988 Walker published *Richard Wright, Daemonic Genius: A Portrait of the Man, A Critical Look at His Work*.

In 1968, she founded the Institute for the Study of the History, Life, and Culture of Black People. She worked as director of the Institute, renamed the Margaret Walker Research Center in her honor, for eleven years. She also encouraged the teaching and learning of Black Studies. Margaret Walker Alexander died on November 30, 1998, in Chicago, Illinois.

# For My People

For my people everywhere singing their slave songs
   repeatedly: their dirges and their ditties and their
   blues and jubilees, praying their prayers nightly to
   an unknown god, bending their knees humbly to an
   unseen power;

For my people lending their strength to the years, to the
   gone years and the now years and the maybe years,
   washing ironing cooking scrubbing sewing mending
   hoeing plowing digging planting pruning patching
   dragging along never gaining never reaping never
   knowing and never understanding.

For my playmates in the clay and dust and sand of
   Alabama backyards playing baptizing and preaching
   and doctor and jail and soldier and school and mama
   and cooking and playhouse and concert and store and
   hair and Miss Choomby and company;

For the cramped bewildered years we went to school
   to learn to know the reasons why and the answers
   to and the people who and the places where and the
   days when, in memory of the bitter hours when we
   discovered we were black and poor and small and
   different and nobody cared and nobody wondered and
   nobody understood;

For the boys and girls who grew in spite of these things
   to be Man and Woman, to laugh and dance and
   sing and play and drink their wine and religion and
   success, to marry their playmates and bear children
   and then die of consumption and anemia and lynching;

For my people thronging 47th Street in Chicago and
   Lenox Avenue in New York and Rampart Street in New
   Orleans, lost disinherited dispossessed and happy

people filling the cabarets and taverns and other
people's pockets needing bread and shoes and milk
and land and money and something—something all our
own;

For my people walking blindly spreading joy, losing time
being lazy, sleeping when hungry, shouting when
burdened, drinking when hopeless, tied and shackled
and tangled among ourselves by the unseen creatures
who tower over us omnisciently and laugh;

For my people blundering and groping and floundering
in the dark of churches and schools and clubs and
societies, associations and councils and committees
and conventions, distressed and disturbed and
deceived and devoured by money-hungry glory-craving
leeches, preyed on by facile force of state and fad and
novelty by false prophet and holy believer;

For my people standing staring trying to fashion
a better way from confusion from hypocrisy and
misunderstanding, trying to fashion a world that will
hold all the people, all the faces, all the adams and
eves and their countless generations;

Let a new earth rise. Let another world be born. Let
a bloody peace be written in the sky. Let a second
generation full of courage issue forth; let a people
loving freedom come to growth. Let a beauty full of
healing and a strength of final clenching be the pulsing
in our spirits and our bloos. Let the martial songs be
written, let the dirges disappea. Let a race of men now
rise and take control.

# Lineage

My grandmothers were strong.
They followed plows and bent to toil.
They moved through fields sowing seed.
They touched earth and grain grew.
They were full of sturdiness and singing.
My grandmothers were strong.

My grandmothers are full of memories
Smelling of soap and onions and wet clay
With veins rolling roughly over quick hands
They have many clean words to say.
My grandmothers were strong.
Why am I not as they?

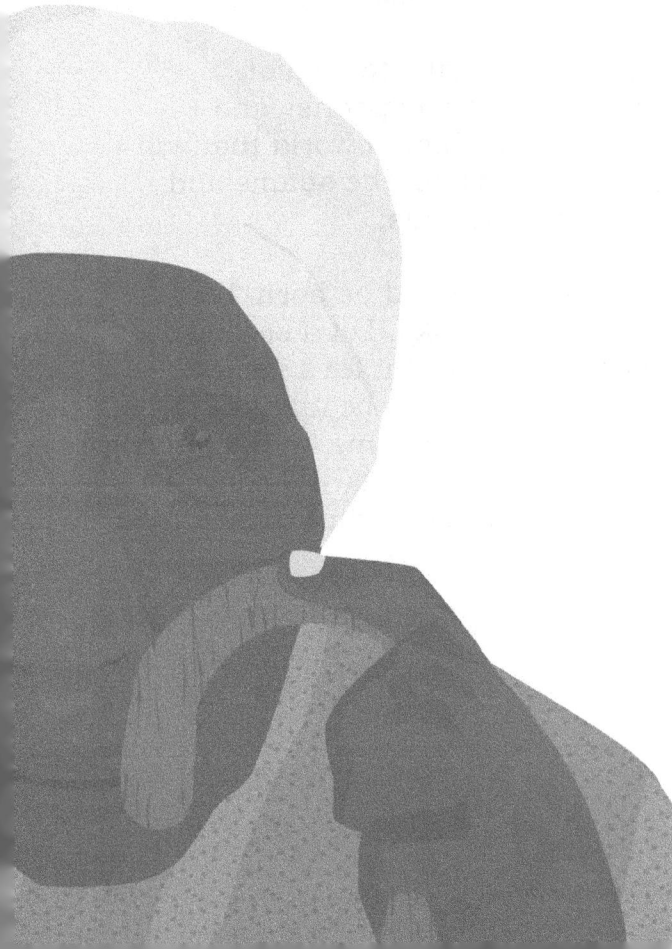

# Birmingham

1.

With the last whippoorwill call of evening
Settling over mountains
Dusk dropping down shoulders of red hills
And red dust of mines
Sifting across somber sky
Setting the sun to rest in a blue blaze of coal fire
And shivering memories of Spring
With raw wind out of woods
And brown straw of last year's needle-shedding-pines
Cushions of quiet underfoot
Violets pushing through early new spring ground
And my winging heart flying across the world
With one bright bird—
Cardinal flashing through thickets—
Memories of my fancy-ridden life
Come home again.

2.

I died today.
In a new and cruel way.
I came to breakfast in my night-dying clothes
Ate and talked and nobody knew
They had buried me yesterday.
I slept outside city limits
Under a little hill of butterscotch brown
With a dusting of white sugar
Where a whistling ghost kept making a threnody
Out of a naked wind.

3.

Call me home again to my coffin bed of soft warm clay.
I cannot bear to rest in frozen wastes
Of a bitter cold and sleeting northern womb.
My life dies best on a southern cross
Carved out of rock with shooting stars to fire
The forge of bitter hate.

# Gwendolyn Brooks

## 1917–2000

Gwendolyn Brooks began writing at a very early age. Her first poems were printed in a community newspaper. When she was 13, one of her poems was published in *American Child*, a children's magazine. Thus began a literary career that would establish Gwendolyn Brooks as one of America's most celebrated poets.

She was the first African-American writer to win the Pulitzer Prize (1950) and the first to be appointed to the American Academy of Arts and Letters (1976). In 1968 she was named Poet Laureate for the state of Illinois. She received a lifetime achievement award from the National Endowment for the Arts, and in 1994 was named Jefferson Lecturer by the National Endowment for the Humanities, the highest honor bestowed by the federal government for work in the humanities. Brooks published more than 20 volumes of poetry and several books of prose, and was the recipient of more than 50 honorary degrees during her long and distinguished literary career.

Gwendolyn Brooks was born in Topeka, Kansas. When she was five weeks old, her family moved to Chicago, where she would spend most of her life. While attending high school, she wrote a column for the *Chicago Defender* and had one of her poems critiqued by poet and novelist James Weldon Johnson.

After graduating from junior college in 1936, Brooks married Henry L. Blakeley II in 1939. She continued to write and attend writing workshops. In 1943, she won the Midwestern Writers' Conference poetry award. Afterward, she gathered nineteen of her poems and submitted them to Harper & Bros. Publishers. The result was the publication of her first volume of poetry, *A Street in Bronzeville*, released in 1945. In 1949, her second volume, *Annie Allen*, was published. It earned her a Pulitzer Prize in 1950. In 1953, a novel, *Maud Martha*, was published, followed by *Bronzeville Boys and Girls* in 1956 and *The Bean Eaters* in 1961. Brooks's body of work continued to grow in the sixties, seventies, and eighties. *We Real Cool* was published in 1966, *The Wall* in 1967, *In the Mecca* in 1968, *Riot* in 1970, *Aloneness* in 1971, and *Beckonings* in 1975. *To Disembark* followed in 1982 and *Children Coming Home* was released in 1991.

Brooks's poems offer insight into Black culture and life. They comment on racism, ethnic identity, social conditions, and the day-to-day existence of Black Americans. Just as Langston Hughes influenced her writing, she influenced and was an example to younger writers such as Don L. Lee (Haki Madhubuti) and Larry Neal. Brooks in turn was inspired and motivated by the confidence, firmness, and fire younger Black poets exuded.

Gwendolyn Brooks continued to write and to present readings of her work until she was overtaken by the illness that caused her death in 2000. "I believe that we should all know each other, we are human carriers of so many pleasurable differences," she said in an interview. "To not know is to doubt, to shrink from, sidestep, or destroy."

# We Real Cool

THE POOL PLAYERS
SEVEN AT THE GOLDEN SHOVEL.

We real cool. We
Left school. We

Lurk late. We
Strike straight. We

Sing sin. We
Thin gin. We

Jazz June. We
Die soon.

# Paul Robeson

That time
we all heard it,
cool and clear,
cutting across the hot grit of the day.
The major Voice.
The adult Voice
forgoing Rolling River,
forgoing tearful tale of bale and barge
and other symptoms of an old despond.
Warning, in music-words
Devout and large,
that we are each other's
harvest:
we are each other's
business:
we are each other's
magnitude and bond.

# Medgar Evers

For Charles Evers

The man whose height his fear improved he
arranged to fear no further. The raw
intoxicated time was time for better birth or a final death.

Old styles, old tempos, all the engagement of
the day—the sedate, the regulated fray—
the antique light, the Moral rose, old gusts,
tight whistlings from the past, the mothballs
in the Love at last our man forswore.

Medgar Evers annoyed confetti and assorted
brands of businessmen's eyes.

The shows came down: to maxims and surprise.
And palsy.

Roaring no rapt arise-ye to the dead, he
leaned across tomorrow. People said that
he was holding clean globes in his hands.

# To Be in Love

To be in love
Is to touch things with a lighter hand.

In yourself you stretch, you are well.

You look at things
Through his eyes.
A Cardinal is red.
A sky is blue.
Suddenly you know he knows too.
He is not there but
You know you are tasting together
The winter, or light spring weather.

His hand to take your hand is overmuch.
Too much to bear.

You cannot look in his eyes
Because your pulse must not say
What must not be said.

When he
Shuts a door—
Is not there—
Your arms are water.

And you are free
With a ghastly freedom.

You are the beautiful half
Of a golden hurt.

You remember and covet his mouth,
To touch, to whisper on.

Oh when to declare
Is certain Death!

Oh when to apprize
Is to mesmerize,

To see fall down, the Column of Gold,
Into the commonest ash.

# Other Pioneer Poets of Note

**Gwendolyn Bennett** (1902–1981), born in Giddings, Texas
Bennett was a leading voice of the Harlem Renaissance. Her poems and illustrations appeared in magazines such as *Opportunity* and *Fire!* A writer and illustrator, she wrote a column that appeared in *Opportunity* and she taught at Howard University in Washington, D.C. Bennett is considered one of the most skilled poets of the Harlem Renaissance.

**Arna Bontemps** (1902–1973), born in Alexandria, Louisiana
Bontemps's poems were first published in *Crisis* magazine in 1924. He soon earned recognition as a novelist, an author of books for children, and a poet. He edited several poetry anthologies, including *The Poetry of the Negro: 1746–1949*, with Langston Hughes, and *Golden Slippers*. In 1943, he became librarian at Fisk University in Nashville, Tennessee, a post he held for many years.

**William Stanley Braithwaite** (1878–1962), born in Boston, Massachusetts
A poet, critic, and anthologist, Braithwaite's poetry used the traditional meters and forms of the nineteenth century. His subjects were general, and did not focus on Black life and culture like those of many contemporary Black poets. His volumes of poetry included *Lyrics of Life and Love* (1904) and *The House of Falling Leaves* (1908). Braithwaite was a professor of literature at Atlanta University.

**Jupitor Hammon** (1720?–1800?), born in Long Island, New York
Hammon was a contemporary of Lucy Terry and Phillis Wheatley. His poem "An Evening Thought: Salvation By Christ, with Penetential Cries" was published in 1760. A slave for all of his life, Hammon also had a number of other poems published, including "Address to Phillis Wheatley" (1778) and "An Essay on the Ten Virgins" (1779).

**Robert Hayden** (1913–1982), born in Detroit, Michigan
In 1976, Hayden was appointed consultant in poetry to the Library of Congress, the first African American to be so honored. Considered by some to be one of America's finest poets, many of Hayden's poems focused on African-American history. His published work includes *Heart Shape in the Dust* (1940), *Selected Poems* (1966), and *Works in the Morning Time* (1970). Hayden taught at Fisk University and at the University of Michigan.

**George Moses Horton** (1797?–1883?), born in Northampton County, North Carolina When Horton's volume of poems, *The Hope of Liberty*, was published in 1829, it was the first book of African-American poetry released in more than fifty years. A slave who began creating poems and rhymes before he could read or write, Horton's second volume of poetry, *The Poetical Works of George M. Horton, The Colored Bard of North Carolina*, was published in 1845. Unlike the African-American poets before him, some of Horton's poems addressed the issue of slavery.

**Fenton Johnson** (1888–1958), born in Chicago, Illinois
Some of Johnson's earlier poetry, written in Black dialect, was influenced by Paul Laurence Dunbar. He used folk forms such as spirituals and blues. Langston Hughes, James Weldon Johnson, and Sterling Brown would also draw from these forms during the 1920s and 1930s. Johnson's first volume of poetry, *A Little Dreaming*, was published in 1913. *Visions of the Dusk* (1915) and *Songs of the Soul* (1916) followed.

**Helene Johnson** (1907–1995), born in Boston, Massachusetts
Johnson was the youngest of the Harlem Renaissance poets. At age 19, one of her poems won honorable mention in *Opportunity* magazine's annual contest for African-American writers. Many of the two dozen or so poems she wrote during the Harlem Renaissance appeared in magazines such as *Vanity Fair*, *Fire!* and *Opportunity*, as well as in anthologies.

**Anne Spencer** (1882–1975), born in Bramwell, Virginia
Spencer worked for many years as the librarian at Dunbar High School in Lynchburg, Virginia. Like Georgia Douglas Johnson, her home in Lynchburg was a meeting place for many Black poets of the Harlem Renaissance. Spencer never published a volume of poetry, but many of her poems have appeared in leading magazines and anthologies.

**Lucy Terry** (1730–1821), born in Africa
"Bars Fight," a poem commemorating a Native American attack on a Deerfield, Massachussetts haying party, is considered the first known poem written by an African American. Published in 1855, it was Terry's only published poem. Terry was also recognized for her speaking ability and determination to fight for her rights.

**Melvin B. Tolson** (1900–1966), born in Moberly, Missouri
Tolson was named Poet Laureate of the West African nation of Liberia in 1947. *The Libretto for the Republic of Liberia*, completed for Liberia's centennial in 1956, was perhaps his most ambitious work. He taught at Wiley College in Marshall, Texas, and at Langston University in Oklahoma. His volumes of poetry include *Rendezvous with America* (1944) and *Harlem Gallery* (1965). Tolson was writer-in-residence at Tuskegee Institute when he died in 1966.

**Jean Toomer** (1894–1967), born in Washington, D.C.
After the 1923 release of *Cane*, a book that used poetry and prose to address impressions of Black life in the South, Toomer was considered one of the brightest young writers of the Harlem Renaissance. He wrote a number of other poems, short stories and plays, but *Cane* was his greatest triumph, and he was never able to create a work of that magnitude again.

**James Monroe Whitfield** (1822–1871), born in Exeter, New Hampshire
Whitfield's poems frequently appeared in Frederick Douglass's newspaper, *North Star*. In 1853, Whitfield, who worked as a barber, published his first col- lection, *America and Other Poems*. A leader in the anti-slavery movement, Whitfield is considered one of the most accomplished African-American anti-slavery poets.

# Selected Bibliography

Adoff, Arnold, *The Poetry of Black America, Anthology of the 20th Century*, HarperCollins, New York, NY, 1973.

Bontemps, Arna, *American Negro Poetry*, Hill and Wang, New York, NY, 1963.

Braxton, M. Joanne, *The Collected Poems of Paul Laurence Dunbar*, The University Press of Virginia, Charlottesville, VA, 1993.

Brooks, Gwendolyn, *A Street in Bronzeville*, Harper & Row, New York, NY, 1945.

Brooks, Gwendolyn, *Annie Allen*, Harper & Brothers, New York, 1949; reprinted Greenwood Press, Westport, CT, 1989.

Brooks, Gwendolyn, *Aloneness*, Broadside Press, Detroit, MI, 1971.

Brown, Sterling A., Davis, Arthur P., & Lee, Ulysses, *The Negro Caravan*, Citadel Press, Secaucus, NJ, 1941.

Cullen, Countee, *Caroling Dusk*, Harper & Brothers, New York, NY, 1927.

Davis, Arthur P., & Redding, Saunders, *Calvacade: Negro American Writing from 1760 to the Present*, Houghton Mifflin, Boston, MA, 1971.

Dunbar, Paul Laurence, *Lyrics of the Hearthside*, Dodd, Mead, Inc., New York, NY, 1913.

Early, Gerald, *My Soul's High Song: The Collected Writings of Countee Cullen, Voice of the Harlem Renaissance*, Anchor Books, New York, NY, 1991.

Graham, MaryEmma, *The Complete Poems of Frances E. W. Harper*, Oxford University Press, New York, NY, 1988.

Harper, Michael S. & Walton, Anthony, *The Vintage Book of African-American Poetry*, Vintage Books, A Division of Random House, Inc., New York, NY, 2000.

Harper, Michael, *The Collected Poems of Sterling A. Brown*, Harper and Row, New York, NY, 1980.

Hughes, Langston & Bontemps, Arna, *The Poetry of the Negro*, Doubleday, New York, NY, 1949.

Hughes, Langston, *New Negro Poets*, Indiana University Press, Bloomington, IN, 1964.

Hughes, Langston, *The Collected Poems of Langston Hughes*, Alfred A. Knopf, Inc., New York, NY, 1994.

Johnson, Georgia Douglas, *Share My World*, A Book of Poems, 1962.

Johnson, James Weldon, *God's Trombones: Seven Negro Sermons in Verse*, Viking Press, 1927, New York, NY, reprinted, 1976.

Lomax, Alan, & Raoul, Abdal, *Three Thousand Years of Black Poetry*, Dodd and Mead, New York, NY, 1969.

Mason, Julia, *The Poems of Phillis Wheatley*, Revised and Enlarged Edition, University of North Carolina Press, Chapel Hill, NC, 1989.

McKay, Claude, *Selected Poems of Claude McKay*, Harvest, Harcourt, New York, NY, 1953.

Robinson, William H., *Early Black American Poets*, William C. Brown/ McGraw-Hill, New York, NY, 1969.

Shields, John C., *The Collected Works of Phillis Wheatley*, Oxford University Press, New York, NY, 1988.

Turner, Darwin, *Black American Literature: Poetry*, Charles E. Merrill Publishing Co., Columbus, OH, 1969.

Walker, Margaret, *For My People*, Yale University Press, New Haven, CT, 1942.

Walker, Margaret, *This Is My Century: New and Collected Poems*, University of Georgia Press, Athens, GA, 1990.

# Acknowledgments

The poems reprinted in this book were obtained and used with permission from the sources listed below. Every effort has been made to trace ownership of all copyrighted material and to secure the necessary authorization to reprint each selection. In the event of any question regarding the fair use of any materials, or any inadvertent error, the publisher will be happy to make the necessary correction in future printings.

"An Hymn to the Evening," and "To S.M., A Young African Painter, on Seeing His Works" by Phillis Wheatley.

"Bury Me in a Free Land," "The Slave Mother," and "The Slave Auction" by Frances Ellen Harper.

"The Creation" from *God's Trombones* by James Weldon Johnson, copyright 1927, The Viking Press, Inc., renewed copyright 1955 by Grace Nail Johnson. Used by permission of Viking Penguin, a division of Penguin Group (USA). "O Black and Unknown Bards" from *Saint Peter Relates an Incident* by James Weldon Johnson, copyright 1917, 1921, 1935 by James Weldon Johnson, copyright renewed 1963 by Grace Nail Johnson. Used by permission of Viking Penguin, a division of Penguin Group (USA).

"Sympathy," "We Wear the Mask," "Little Brown Baby," and "The Poet" by Paul Laurence Dunbar.

"If We Must Die," "Africa," "America," and "Harlem Shadow" by Claude McKay reprinted courtesy of the Literary Representative for the work of Claude McKay, Schomburg Center for Research in Black Culture, The New York Public Library, Astor, Lenox, and Tilden foundations.

"I Want to Die While You Love Me," "The Heart of a Woman," and "Your World" by Georgia Douglas Johnson.

"Incident" and "Heritage" from *Color* by Countee Cullen, copyright 1925 by Harper & Brothers, copyright renewed 1953 by Ida M. Cullen. "From a Dark Tower" from *Copper Sun* by Countee Cullen, copyright 1927 by Harper & Brothers, copyright renewed 1955 by Ida M. Cullen.

"Mother to Son," "Madam and the Rent Man," "Dream Variations," "I, Too," and "The Negro Speaks of Rivers" from the *Collected Poems of Langston Hughes* by Langston Hughes, copyright 1994 by the Estate of Langston Hughes. Used by permission of Alfred A. Knopf, a division of Random House, Inc.

"After Winter" and "Rain" from *The Collected Poems of Sterling A. Brown*, edited by Michael S. Harper, copyright 1980 by Sterling Brown, reprinted by permission of HarperCollins Publishers Inc. "Strong Men" from *The Collected Poems of Sterling A. Brown*, edited by Michael S. Harper, copyright 1932 Harcourt Brace & Co., renewed 1960 by Sterling Brown. Originally appeared in *Southern Road*, reprinted by permission of HarperCollins Publishers Inc.

"For My People," "Lineage," and "Birmingham" by Margaret Walker, from the estate of Margaret Walker Alexander.

"We Real Cool," "Medgar Evers," "Paul Robeson," and "To Be in Love" by Gwendolyn Brooks reprinted by consent of Brooks Permissions.

Cover design by Carol Jenkins-Cooper, Jenkins Graphics.

## About the Author

**Wade Hudson** is an author and publisher. He is president and CEO of Just Us Books, Inc., an independent publisher of books for children and young adults. Among his 30 published books for children and young adults are *Book of Black Heroes from A to Z*, *Jamal's Busy Day*, *Pass It On: African American Poetry for Children*, *Powerful Words: More Than Two Hundred Years of Extraordinary Writing by African Americans*, *It's Church Going Time*, *Feelings I Love to Share* and *Friends I Love to Meet*. He has received a New Jersey Stephen Crane Literary Award, The Ida B. Wells Institutional Leadership Award (2008), presented by the Center for Black Literature and the Madame C. J. Walker Legacy Award (2012) given by the Zora Neale Hurston-Richard Wright Foundation. He has also been inducted into the International Literary Hall of Fame for Writers of African Descent. His website is http://wadehudson-authorpublisher.com

## About the Illustrator

**Stephan J. Hudson** is a graphic artist and photographer. A graduate of Rowan University in New Jersey, where he received a bachelor's degree in graphic arts, Stephan operates his own photography studio, 2ndchapterphoto located in East Orange, NJ and a artist imprint, "froM tHe xRt LLC". He is also a book designer whose photos and artwork have been featured in the titles *Langston's Legacy: 101 Ways to Celebrate the Life and Work of Langston Hughes*, *Prayers for the Smallest Hands* and *We Rise, We Resist, We Raise Our Voices*. *Poetry from the Masters: The Pioneers* is his first book collaboration with his father, Wade Hudson. For more information about Stephan and his work visit his website at www.iAmSHphotography.com

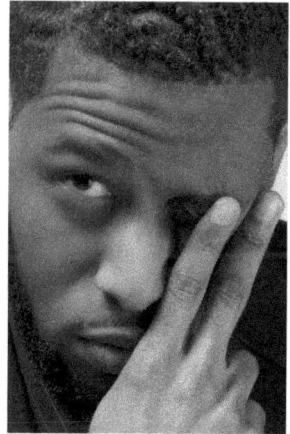

www.ingramcontent.com/pod-product-compliance
Lightning Source LLC
Chambersburg PA
CBHW071416040426
42445CB00012BA/1175